The Edge of Peace

Drama by

SUZAN ZEDER

Dramatic Publishing Company
Woodstock, Illinois • Australia • New Zealand • South Africa

For inquiries concerning all other rights, contact:
Bret Adams, Ltd.
448 44th Street
New York, NY 10036 • Phone: (212) 765-5630

ISBN: 978-1-58342-911-2

IMPORTANT BILLING AND CREDIT REQUIREMENTS

All producers of the play *must* give credit to the author of the play in all programs distributed in connection with performances of the play and in all instances in which the title of the play appears for purposes of advertising, publicizing or otherwise exploiting the play and/or a production. The name of the author *must* also appear on a separate line, on which no other name appears, immediately following the title, and *must* appear in size of type not less than fifty percent (50%) the size of the title type. Biographical information on the author, if included in the playbook, may be used in all programs. *In all programs this notice must appear:*

"Produced by special arrangement with
THE DRAMATIC PUBLISHING COMPANY, INC., of Woodstock, Illinois."

In addition, all producers of the play must include the following acknowledgment on the title page of all programs distributed in connection with performances of the play and on all advertising and promotional materials:

"*The Edge of Peace* was originally commissioned by Seattle Children's Theatre and developed in association with The University of Texas at Austin."

The Edge of Peace

Is dedicated to my friend and collaborator
Linda Hartzell

And to Seattle Children's Theatre
My companions on this long road to Ware

The world premiere of *The Edge of Peace* in February of 2013 was a collaborative production between Seattle Children's Theatre and The Department of Theatre and Dance at the B. Iden Payne Theatre at The University of Texas at Austin.

CAST

Tuc .... Robert Schleifer
Voice.. Dan Lendzian
Nell Hicks .... Franchelle Stewart Dorn
Buddy Ricks... Nate Kelderman
Clovis P. Eudy .... Todd Jefferson Moore
Alma Ward .... Antoinette Robinson
Izzy Ricks.. Therese Diekhans
June Ricks .... Liz Kimball
Margaret.. Suzanne Bouchard
Girl .... Alexis Scott
Soldier/Ricky Ricks .... Kyle Cotton

PRODUCTION STAFF

Director .... Linda Hartzell
Lighting Designer .... Rachel Atkinson
Costume Designer.................. Hope MacRoberts Bennett
Stage Manager .... Rusty Cloyes
Scenic Designer .... Jeff Kurihara
Technical Director...................................... Dave Vieira
Sound Designer.. Chris R. Walker

AUTHOR'S NOTES

The Edge of Peace is the end of a very long road that began for me over 30 years ago when the character of Tuc first appeared in the theatre of my mind and astonished me when he spoke in sign language. This play represents the third and final play of a trilogy that also includes *Mother Hicks* and *The Taste of Sunrise*. All three plays are set in the same tiny town of Ware, Ill. and each play captures the essence of a pivotal area of American history, the Roaring '20s, The Great Depression of the 1930s and the last days of World War II, as reflected in thc lives, loves and losses of the townspeople of Ware.

All three plays have at their core seminal issues of Deaf and hearing cultures, courageous young protagonists and, of course, Tuc, the Deaf character who led me on this journey. In *The Taste of Sunrise*, Tuc's deafness is both pathology and promise as young Tuc is caught between the strictures of "oralism," which forced Deaf children to try to speak and read lips, and the depth of expression of sign language. In *Mother Hicks*, Tuc's deafness renders him an outsider, but here in *The Edge of Peace*, Tuc, as both person and Postman, is at the very center of his community. He has become the town's primary source of communication with one another and with their loved ones far away at War. He is the emotional fulcrum of Ware.

In this play, each of the characters has a different method of communication with Tuc, and it is important to understand the differences in production. Buddy relies on broad gestures and a kind of "home sign" they have constructed through their friendship. He also finger spells. Clovis, Tuc's employer, exchanges written notes with Tuc. June and Alma speak slowly, enunciate clearly and rely on lip reading and simple gestures. Izzy, still as insensitive as ever, simply speaks louder. Nell and Girl have been taught sign by Tuc. They use "home sign," a simplified gestural language, with ease and fluidity.

Margaret, a professional Deaf recruiter, uses American Sign Language (ASL) with professional efficiency, and Tuc responds in kind. In their one scene together, Margaret both speaks and signs. If this were "really" happening, she would not speak, but since this is theatre, I have taken the liberty to have her speak her own words, while the character of Voice voices for Tuc here and throughout the play. Voice has, perhaps, the most complex relationship with Tuc. He is much more than an interpreter of Tuc's signs for an audience; he is Tuc's alter ego, that part of Tuc which exists in the hearing world. Tuc and Voice are one being.

Because Deafness is at the heart of this play, and all the plays of the trilogy, it is vitally important to me and to any eventual production that Tuc be played by a Deaf actor. I cannot overemphasize this point. To cast a hearing actor in this role is ethically, politically and aesthetically wrong! I have been told by some producers that they have "no choice" but to cast a hearing actor in this role, to which I reply, "You DO have a choice. You can choose to do a different play!"

The Edge of Peace is about more than Deafness. It is a play about home: about coming home, staying home and leaving home, in a time when the adventure and danger of the world threatens and beckons. It has been my honor and my privilege to have had all three of these plays in my life for over three decades. They have taught me everything I know about the courage of young people who survive desperate times with dignity and humor, about the beauty of a language that is silent, about the humanity of a community capable of change. I offer this play, and all these plays, to you with all my heart.

Suzan Zeder, Santa Fe, 2014

The Edge of Peace

CHARACTERS

TUC: Postman and mechanic, mid-30s, Deaf.

VOICE: Tuc's alter ego and the manifestation of his voice in the hearing world.

BUDDY RICKS: The little brother left behind, 11.

NELL HICKS: The woman who lives on Dug Hill, known to some as Mother Hicks.

RICKY RICKS: Missing in action.

CLOVIS P. EUDY: Shopkeeper and air raid warden of the town.

IZZY RICKS: War mother, 60s.

JUNE RICKS: War bride, early 20s.

ALMA WARD: War wife, 40s.

MARGARET: Recruiter for Goodyear Company, 39.

GIRL: WASP (Women's Air Force Service Pilot), 23.

SOLDIER: Prisoner of war, also plays Ricky.

RADIO VOICE

PRESIDENT'S VOICE: Voice of President Franklin Delano Roosevelt.

TIME

1945

SETTING

The road: The road through Ware. Tuc's mail route. Soldiers come home from the war along this road … or don't.

Porches: Houses of the women left behind. Peaked roof lines and window frames. Blue stars in the windows of Izzy's, June's and Alma's houses signify family members in battle. Gold stars for soldiers killed in action. There are no gold stars in Ware … yet.

The store: Clovis P. Eudy's General Mercantile. A counter, a barrel full of peanuts and a huge map with pins for all the townspeople stationed overseas. A spotter's post is on the roof.

Dug Hill: A tarpaper shack where Mother Hicks has lived all these years. On the front porch is a shortwave radio. There are cages for critters, an outdoor cook fire and maybe a rocking chair.

The foxhole: On a battlefield far away and later in memory.

The campsite: In the woods on the west slope of Dug Hill. A tree stump.

The Edge of Peace

ACT I

PROLOGUE

AT RISE: *Home front / battlefront. A fragmentary set reveals multiple locations: the store, Dug Hill and the road. TUC enters, riding his bike and ringing a bell that he cannot hear. TUC stops and dismounts as VOICE enters. VOICE and TUC give each other a brief nod. TUC signs. VOICE speaks.*

TUC. This town is Ware
W. A .R. E.
Streets, three
Houses, fifteen
Farms, ten
Churches, four
A garage, sawmill and a store
Not much more.

(TUC points to the spotter's post above CLOVIS P. EUDY's store.)

TUC *(cont'd)*. Down in town a boy waits
While he waits he dreams of war.

(Lights up on BUDDY RICKS in the cockpit of an imaginary plane.)

BUDDY. Deep into enemy territory, ace pilot Buddy Ricks grabs the joystick of his F4F Wildcat and pulls up hard! He shouts to copilot: "We're taking flack from the ack ack!"

(Lights up on NELL HICKS at the shortwave radio on Dug Hill.)

TUC. Up on Dug Hill
A woman sits at a radio
Listening to a language she doesn't know.
Spoken from somewhere she will never go.

RADIO VOICE. *Hier ist Radio Berlin mit dem Programm "Anrufe Nach Hause."*

(The radio goes to static.)

NELL *(smacks the radio)*. Blast!

TUC. Far away,
A soldier sits in a foxhole all alone,
Waiting for the battle to begin.
While he waits, he dreams of home.

(Lights up on RICKY RICKS in the foxhole on the other side of the world.)

RICKY. Dear Momma, last night I dreamed of your lemon vinegar pie. It was so sweet and tart that I made little smacking sounds in my sleep.

TUC *(as VOICE hands him a mail sack)*. I am Tuc,
Mechanic, farmer and postman
For this town.
The government says Deaf men cannot soldiers be.
So, this is a town of women, children, old men and me.
We are all waiting, waiting, waiting for peace.

(TUC delivers three letters to BUDDY, IZZY and JUNE RICKS.)

BUDDY. Thank you, Tuc.

IZZY. Thank you, Tuc.

JUNE. Thank you, Tuc.

TUC. It is 1944.
The whole world is at war.

(Lights up on the foxhole. Sounds of gunfire.)

IZZY. It's from Ricky!

RICKY. Dear Momma, they say we're shipping out, headed somewhere really cold.

(CLOVIS enters with a map.)

CLOVIS. Belgium.

JUNE. It's from Ricky!

RICKY. Oh, Juney Blue, I miss you so bad it hurts! I dream about you every night and wake up kissing my own arm.

CLOVIS. Bastonge.

BUDDY. It's from Ricky!

CLOVIS. Battle of the Bulge.

(Explosion. Gunfire intensifies. As BUDDY, JUNE and IZZY read RICKY's letters, we hear their voices and RICKY's voice, until RICKY's voice drops out, and they continue to read his words.)

RICKY & BUDDY. "We started taking fire last night."

RICKY & JUNE. "It's so cold here my feet keep freezing in my boots … "

RICKY & IZZY. "My foxhole feels like an icebox and I haven't had a hot shower in two months!"

RICKY & BUDDY. "I started laying down cover fire so we could dig in but the snow was packed hard as cement!"

BUDDY. "I keep firing and my heart is hammering. I can feel the bullets whizzing past me, and everyone is yelling … "

RICKY & BUDDY. "Keep your head down!"

BUDDY. "So, Gus and I start running."

BUDDY & RICKY. "RUN!"

(A mortar shell explodes in light and smoke.)

RICKY. I can't see you! I can't hear you! I can't …

(Explosion. Pandemonium. RICKY disappears in a blinding flash.)

IZZY. "Don't worry about me, Momma."

JUNE. "Don't worry about me, June."

BUDDY. "Don't worry about me, Buddy."

(TUC rings the bell. He hands IZZY a yellow envelope. She reads the telegram aloud.)

IZZY. "I regret to inform you that your son, Private First Class Richard Ricks, was reported missing in action near Bastogne on December 18, 1944. If further details or other information of his status are received, you will be promptly notified."

(Lights out on CLOVIS, IZZY, JUNE and BUDDY. TUC steps into a spotlight.)

TUC. Three months pass.
His family waits day after day after day.
Their hearts break from the silence
Half a world away.

(TUC and VOICE exchange a glance and exit.)

SCENE 1

(The store—morning. Lights up on BUDDY in the spotter's post above CLOVIS' store. He is flying an imaginary plane in an imaginary battle.)

BUDDY. We're taking flack from the ack ack! Let 'em have it! Kerpow! We're hit! The right engine's on fire. Take it easy, we've still got the left one!

(Battle sounds stop abruptly as CLOVIS enters, switches on a light and opens his shop. CLOVIS grabs a broom and raps on the trap door that leads to the spotter's post above his store.)

CLOVIS. Buddy Ricks, are you up there again?

BUDDY. Yes, sir.

CLOVIS. I'm not even open yet, how did you get in?

BUDDY. You gave me a key, remember, in case I needed to take a night shift in the spotter's post.

CLOVIS. You up there alone?

BUDDY. Kind of, sort of …

CLOVIS. Do you have that dog up there with you?

BUDDY. He's my copilot.

CLOVIS. That dog is older than dirt and heavy as sin. He better not be messing up my spotter's post.

BUDDY. No, sir, he's housebroke … mostly. He just makes bad smells sometimes.

CLOVIS. That dog is a 45 pound gasbag.

BUDDY. Good thing we got this.

(BUDDY pokes his head through the trap door. He is wearing a gas mask.)

CLOVIS. You put that away. That's not a toy; it is U.S. government property. You had breakfast yet?

BUDDY. No, sir, I left before my momma was up.

CLOVIS. I got pickled eggs down here and some jerky.

(BUDDY climbs down the ladder. CLOVIS fishes an egg out of a large jar with a long handled spoon.)

CLOVIS *(cont'd)*. So, what have you got?

BUDDY. Surveillance Report, April 5, 1945, Ware, Illinois, Civilian Defense Station 10476. Junior Lieutenant Buddy Ricks reporting: "Absolutely nothing happened!"

CLOVIS.At ease!

BUDDY. Just like yesterday and the day before and the day before that! Mr. Eudy, don't you wish just once SOMETHING would happen?

CLOVIS. Nope.

BUDDY. Over there, where Ricky is, things happen all the time! Ace fighter pilot Smokey Joe Foss shot down five German planes! FIVE in just one day! *(Makes the sounds of shooting.)* POW … POW … POW … POW … POW … YEowwwwwww. BOOOM ! CRASH! How many kills do you suppose Ricky got?

CLOVIS. How many what?

BUDDY. Kills, how many kills do you think Ricky's got?

CLOVIS. Buddy, Ricky was in the infantry …

BUDDY. IS … Ricky IS in the infantry.

(TUC enters, lugging a large cash register. CLOVIS grabs a small pad and writes a note to him.)

CLOVIS. Fixed?

(TUC nods "yes.")

CLOVIS *(cont'd)*. How?

(TUC writes on CLOVIS' pad.)

CLOVIS *(cont'd, reading)*. "The machine told my fingers what to do." *(Scribbles.)* "I've tried to fix that blasted thing for a week and you do it in one hour!"

(TUC writes a reply.)

CLOVIS *(cont'd, reading)*. "I know how to listen."

(BUDDY runs to TUC and signs in an animated gestural 'home sign' as he speaks. TUC reads BUDDY's lips.)

BUDDY. We goin' fishin' today, Tuc?

(TUC shakes his head "no.")

BUDDY *(cont'd)*. But the crappies and blue gills is running.

(TUC indicates that he has to work.)

BUDDY *(cont'd)*. You work ALL the time. *(Finger spells.)* N. O. F. A. I. R.

CLOVIS *(scribbling on the pad)*. "Mail train late?"

(TUC nods "yes.")

CLOVIS *(cont'd, scribbling)*. "How come?"

(TUC draws a question mark. TUC grabs his mail sack and exits.)

BUDDY. Mr. Eudy, can you give me a job? You know, like for money?

CLOVIS. Why?

BUDDY. Mz. Ward just lost her job at the Goodyear plant, and June's worried she could lose hers, too. And if June loses her job, she'll have to move in with us, and sleep in my room, and I'll have to sleep out in the doghouse with Old Watch. So, I need a job!

CLOVIS. What could you do?

BUDDY. I could count peanuts. Every morning, I could see how many peanuts you have in the barrel and then when people eat them, they could pay a penny apiece and I could collect the money!

CLOVIS. Peanuts are free.

BUDDY. Then how are you going to pay me?

CLOVIS. Let's just hope June doesn't lose her job.

BUDDY. I'm going back to the spotter's post. If my momma comes, promise you won't tell her I'm here?

CLOVIS. If she asks me, I'm telling her you're up there!

BUDDY. But, Mr. Eudy, it's Monday and every Monday she makes me go to the war office in Jonesboro and we check the lists to see if Ricky's name is there. Last week they told her that soldiers named Ricks was discharged to Alabama, Indiana and Ohio, but none to Illinois!

CLOVIS. How's she holding up?

BUDDY. She cries almost every night. I hear her through the wall. I don't know what to do. If I talk about Ricky, it makes her sad and if I don't, it makes her mad.

CLOVIS. Just do what you can.

BUDDY. I tell her, "Ricky's not lost! He's somewhere; the Army just doesn't know where." I saw this newsreel of soldiers coming back from Iwo Jima and I swear one of them looked just like Ricky.

CLOVIS. Come here, Buddy.

(CLOVIS leads BUDDY to the map.)

CLOVIS *(cont'd)*. Now, here … this is Belgium, where Ricky was in the Battle of the Bulge. And way over here, this is Iwo Jima. Now, what do you think?

BUDDY *(changing the subject)*. Can we do an aircraft drill again today?

CLOVIS. Buddy, you've got all those planes memorized backwards and forwards. Besides, the Civil Air Patrol says we won't be needing to do drills anymore.

(There is the sound of barking in the spotter's post.)

CLOVIS *(cont'd)*. Buddy, you left that dog up there all alone!

(BUDDY grabs the long handled spoon and runs up the ladder.)

BUDDY. I told you, Old Watch is a good dog …

(BUDDY disappears through the trap door.)

BUDDY *(cont'd)*. Oh, NO! Old Watch! Bad dog! Bad dog!

CLOVIS.What did he do?

BUDDY. Nothin'!

CLOVIS. Did that dog make a mess in my spotter's post?

BUDDY. Uhhh, nope! No mess up here. Not anymore!

(BUDDY can be seen catapulting something out of the spotter's post with the spoon.)

BUDDY *(cont'd)*. Bombs away!

(JUNE enters.)

JUNE. Mr. Eudy, what's that flying off the roof of your store?

CLOVIS. You don't even want to know, June.

JUNE. Is Buddy here?

CLOVIS *(simultaneously)*. Yes?

BUDDY *(simultaneously)*. NO!

JUNE. Buddy, are you going to Jonesboro with your momma this morning?

BUDDY. Not if I can help it.

(BUDDY scrambles down the ladder.)

JUNE. Come on, Buddy, she needs someone to go with her. She's always so sad when she comes back.

BUDDY. Hey, June, my scout troop is doing another scrap drive. You got any nylon stockings, rubber girdles, bacon grease, tin foil or shovels?

JUNE. I don't think so.

BUDDY. Franklin Delano Roosevelt himself says that you can turn your old junk into fighting weapons: 200 nylon stocking and 36 girdles can make 50 powder bags, a pound of bacon grease makes enough ammo for 30 bullets and one old shovel will help make four hand grenades!

JUNE. I don't eat bacon, I don't have an old shovel and I doubt seriously that the president of the United States is interested in my underwear.

BUDDY. He is! He says EVERY citizen must do his part, no matter how small!

JUNE. Buddy, I've got something important to ask you. Were you sneaking around my house in the middle of the night?

BUDDY. Why would I do something like that?

JUNE. I got home from the night shift at the factory dead tired at about midnight, and I woke up at 2 a.m. and I swear someone was watching me through my bedroom window.

BUDDY. I am not a peeper!

JUNE. Your momma said that you sneak out at night.

BUDDY. I'm on patrol. Besides, Ricky always used to sneak out. He told Momma he was sleepwalking, but he wasn't.

(BUDDY returns to the spotter's post.)

JUNE. And she fell for that?

(IZZY enters.)

IZZY. Who fell for what?

(BUDDY slams the trap door shut.)

JUNE. Mother Ricks, I'll go to Jonesboro with you today, if you like.

IZZY. Thank you, dear, but Buddy always likes to go with me and I'd hate to disappoint him. Clovis, do you have gasoline today?

CLOVIS. Yep! First time all week!

JUNE. I brought you my ration coupon. You almost ran out of gas last week.

(ALMA WARD enters.)

ALMA. If you're going to Jonesboro today, Izzy, you better be prepared for a wait.

IZZY. Morning, Alma. What's the matter?

ALMA. I was on my roadkill run this morning in Hosiah's hearse, and I'd just picked up two coyotes, a fox and a raccoon.

IZZY. Alma! How can you put those nasty things in your automobile?

ALMA. I keep them in a coffin.

IZZY. Whatever for?

ALMA. Taxidermy! If anyone ever actually dies around here, we're going to need a mortician. I've got to practice! The military police were not amused when they made me pop open that coffin.

IZZY. Police?

ALMA. They're stopping all the cars, looking in trunks. It is all because of the escape.

IZZY. Escape?

CLOVIS. It was on the radio. One of the German prisoners escaped from the POW camp at Pomona. He was working the apple crop at the Sitter Farm.

IZZY. Don't that just chap you? I am sure Ralph Sitter would rather be picking his own apples himself. But no, he's all the way over in Egypt, Italy or God-knows-somewhere-awful.

ALMA. They stopped the Jonesboro bus right behind me.

IZZY. I hear they've set up a regular Hilton hotel for the prisoners at that old army camp. They've got clean clothes, hot meals, they even have a doctor on staff that sees them regular.

ALMA. Some of them were wounded before they got here.

IZZY. Well, isn't that a pity? Our boys are over there lying in ditches, while we got German soldiers rampaging all over town!

CLOVIS. June, do you suppose that's who you saw at your window?

(The trap door flies open and BUDDY scrambles down the ladder.)

BUDDY. Holy moley! We got ourselves a genuine German on the loose!

IZZY. Buddy Ricks! So, that's where you are!

(NELL enters.)

NELL. Excuse me, Mr. Eudy.

(Instantly, everyone is quiet.)

NELL *(cont'd)*. I wonder if you might have one of these? *(Holds up a radio tube.)*

CLOVIS. That for a shortwave, Mz. Hicks?

NELL. Yes.

CLOVIS. I think I've got some right back here.

(CLOVIS exits to a backroom. There is a beat of tense silence.)

NELL. The Jonesboro bus is late.

ALMA. There's a roadblock just outside of town, probably be there half the day. Are you going to Jonesboro?

NELL. Near there.

ALMA. Izzy, aren't you headed that way? Maybe you could …

IZZY. Well, I'm not sure there'd be … room. I've got a lot of …

NELL. I'll wait for the bus.

(After a chilly beat she looks at IZZY.)

NELL *(cont'd)*. Sorry to hear about your boy.

BUDDY. He ain't dead, just missing.

CLOVIS. Just one left. That'll be 35 cents. Bus might be a while. You're welcome to wait in here.

NELL. I'll go another day.

BUDDY. Excuse me, Mz. Hicks, but my scout troop is doing a scrap drive. You got any nylon stockings, rubber girdles, bacon grease, tin foil or shovels I can have?

NELL. Sorry.

BUDDY. Franklin Delano Roosevelt himself says that you can make 50 powder bags from 200 nylon … stockings … and … 36 … girdles …

NELL *(gives BUDDY a withering look)*. Sorry.

(NELL exits.)

IZZY. Don't you know better than to ask Nell Hicks for anything for the war effort?

ALMA. Now, Izzy …

IZZY. Back when I was selling war bonds, I hiked all the way up Dug Hill and she turned me down flat and when I said, "Nell Hicks, don't you believe in supporting the war effort?" And she turned to me, big as life, and said, "The only thing I support about any war is having it over!" Downright unpatriotic, that's what I say!

JUNE *(bursting out laughing)*. I just can't believe you asked her for a girdle!

BUDDY. It's kind of a shame she didn't go with us to Jonesboro, maybe she could do a spell on the gas tank to keep us from running out.

ALMA. Buddy! You know that witch talk is nonsense!

BUDDY. Some of the kids in school sneak up there at night and listen at her window.

IZZY. You stay away from Dug Hill.

BUDDY. They hear some kind of foreign talk.

ALMA. You leave that woman in peace!

(TUC enters with a large sack of mail.)

CLOVIS. Finally!

BUDDY *(speaks and uses gestural home signs)*. Hey, Tuc, you was on the road, you see anybody that looked, you know … foreign?

(TUC shakes his head. TUC hands CLOVIS a stack of letters. JUNE crosses to TUC.)

JUNE. Tuc, I brought this for you from the Goodyear Plant. It's an application for a job as a mechanic.

(JUNE hands TUC a piece of paper.)

JUNE *(cont'd)*. Look, it says, "Deaf workers welcome to apply."

(TUC thanks her and puts the application in his pocket.)

CLOVIS. Alma, you got a card from Girl! It's postmarked Sweetwater, Texas, Avenger Field.

BUDDY. Is she flying again?

ALMA. You know, Girl. If it's got wings, she's flying it.

IZZY. I keep expecting there will be mail from Ricky.

CLOVIS. And a letter from Hosiah for you, Alma, postmarked EGYPT!

ALMA. Army must be running low on morticians.

IZZY. Two in one day, Alma! How … fortunate.

BUDDY. Anything for us, Mr. Eudy, anything at all?

JUNE. It's been months, but I just keep hoping and wishing and …

CLOVIS. Well, June, looks like you just got your wish!

JUNE. What?

(Everything stops as CLOVIS hands JUNE a packet of letters.)

CLOVIS. And some for you too, Izzy.

(They hardly dare look.)

JUNE. I recognize his handwriting!

IZZY. Merciful heaven! Buddy, there's even one for you …

BUDDY. Jumping Jehovah! Look at this, Tuc! I told you he wasn't dead!

JUNE. They're from Ricky! They are all from RICKY!

(They are beside themselves with joy. TUC looks closely at BUDDY's letter and gestures to CLOVIS.)

CLOVIS. Izzy, look at the postmark.

IZZY *(crestfallen)*. November, 1944.

JUNE. These letters are five months old … before he even got to Belgium.

IZZY. All these months of nothing and now this!

CLOVIS. That's the Army for you! U.S. mail ought to be more orderly than that!

BUDDY. They're still letters. They're still from Ricky.

IZZY. Clovis, I don't think I'll be going to Jonesboro today. Come along home, Buddy.

BUDDY. But I gotta get Old Watch down from …

CLOVIS. You go along home with your mamma. I'll get him down … somehow.

(IZZY, BUDDY and ALMA exit. JUNE hangs back.)

CLOVIS *(cont'd)*. June, are you all right?

JUNE. I think I'd like to sit here for a while. Home is kind of an empty place right now.

CLOVIS. Would you like a cold Coca-Cola? I've got some in the cooler.

JUNE. That would be nice.

(TUC crosses to JUNE with the coke.)

JUNE *(cont'd)*. Tuc, would you be with me while I read this? When I read Ricky's letters out loud, it's like I'm hearing his voice and it comforts me. You know what I mean?

TUC. No.

JUNE. I'm so afraid he's not coming back. I can't say that to his mother or to Buddy, but I've got to say it to someone. You are the best listener in this town and your can't hear one word I am saying.

(JUNE opens the letter and reads it aloud. As she does, lights come up on RICKY who begins speaking his letter with her.)

RICKY & JUNE. "My dearest June, we move out tomorrow. This is it! The real thing."

(JUNE reads silently as RICKY continues.)

RICKY. I'm not really scared of fighting, that's what they've trained us to do. I'm not scared of dying, because I can't imagine what that would be like. I'm most scared of screwing up, of making some knucklehead mistake that hurts or kills somebody else in my unit. So, if you want to say a prayer or something, don't say one for me, say one for everyone else … OK?

(TUC steps into a spotlight and is joined by VOICE. TUC hands the paper from JUNE to VOICE.)

TUC. "Goodyear Factory in Akron, Ohio, needs experienced mechanic.
Good pay, full benefits.
Deaf workers welcome to apply."

(TUC and VOICE exchange a look.)

TUC *(cont'd)*. These words I think I will never see,
Never think they could mean me.
Akron, I think, is far from home
But this day I write a letter of my own!

(VOICE mimes writing TUC's answers to his questions.)

VOICE. Name …
TUC. Jonas Tucker Jr.
VOICE. Qualifications:
TUC. I can fix anything that moves.

(Lights change.)

SCENE 2

(Lights up on Dug Hill—evening. A tarpaper shack, a campfire and a rocking chair. A porch with a radio on a table. NELL peers under the porch.)

NELL. It ain't no use, no use at all! I can see that lie right through your glassy little eyes! Eyeballs all rolled back, lips curled, foaming at the mouth! You ain't foolin' me one bit!

(TUC enters with his bike. NELL speaks and signs to him in home sign. VOICE enters and voices what TUC signs.)

NELL *(cont'd)*. How far did you take him?

TUC. Far.

NELL. Not far enough, 'cause here he's back again, stiff as a board, splayed out on his backside under my porch.

TUC. Hurt?

NELL. Dead!

TUC. Not again?

NELL. Everyday you take him far as the county line and every night he shows up here again. Next time, stuff him in the luggage compartment on the bus to Jonesboro, see how he gets out of that one!

TUC. Why can't he just stay?

NELL. I told you, Tuc, he's got to learn how to forage for himself. He can't always be sucking around here, rooting in the garbage and living on sour milk and apple peelings.

TUC *(peering under the porch)*. Can I feed him, anyway?

NELL. All right.

(TUC takes a bottle of milk and pours some in a small saucer.)

TUC. You're supposed to be resting!

NELL. I rested all day. All that resting was making me tired! *(Points to the milk.)* Is that good and sour? He won't drink it otherwise.

(TUC sniffs it and makes a face.)

NELL *(cont'd)*. Put it close to his nose, that'll bring him around.

(NELL hands TUC a handful of berries.)

NELL *(cont'd)*. While you're at it, toss in some juniper berries. He loves those little berries.

(TUC puts the berries in the milk and sets the saucer under the porch.)

TUC. You got the letter.

NELL. Finally!

(TUC hands her a letter. She opens it, scans it and crumples it up.)

TUC. Are you going to tell me what it says?

NELL. Don't say nothing I don't already know.

TUC. You need help!

NELL. There ain't no help, you know that.

TUC. You can't do this, up here, alone.

NELL. I have lived here through flood and fire. I have fed myself from this land in plenty and in famine. I have healed every creature that came in need or want. I know what I can and cannot do.

TUC. This is different.

NELL. Not to me. *(Beat.)* Did Clovis Eudy or anyone in the store see this?

(TUC shakes his head "no.")

NELL *(cont'd)*. Good. I don't cotton much to people knowing my business, 'specially not this business! SECRET!

TUC. Secrets are safe with me.

NELL. I know …

(NELL hands TUC three postcards.)

NELL *(cont'd)*. Now, take these back to town with you and mail them! Important! I expect there will be more tomorrow!

TUC. You rest!

NELL. There's no time to rest. *(Tunes her radio.)*

RADIO VOICE. *Hier ist Radio Berlin mit dem Programm "Anrufe Nach Hause." Wir bringen Ihnen die Namen der amerikanischen Soldaten.*

(Lights shift. TUC moves into a spotlight.)

TUC. Late at night. Everyone's asleep.
The boy climbs out his window
To patrol the streets.
I wait, I watch, I follow
To be sure that he is safe.
But on this night I see …

SCENE 3

(The streets—night. Lights up on BUDDY. TUC follows at a distance. VOICE stands in the shadows and voices for TUC.)

BUDDY. April 5, 1945. 10:33 p.m. Night patrol surveillance report. Hey, what's this? *(Finds something on the ground.)* Cigarette butts … three of them. And they still smell smoky. WOW, and this … a gum wrapper! *(Licks the wrapper.)* Still tastes like Juicy Fruit!

(The SOLDIER with a ragged beard wearing a tattered greatcoat steps out of the shadow and follows BUDDY.)

BUDDY *(cont'd)*. Ricky won't believe I really did this all by myself. It will be just like *Terry and the Pirates,* when Terry was sneaking up on a nest of Nazis.

(TUC crosses toward the SOLDIER.)

BUDDY *(cont'd)*. They caught him in their search lights and opened fire.

(There is the sound of gunfire. TUC snaps on a flashlight. The SOLDIER whirls around with his hands in front of his face and lunges at TUC.)

BUDDY *(cont'd)*. Suddenly out of nowhere, a Nazi spy jumps him and wrestles him to the ground. *(Acts out his imaginary fight.)* OOOF … POW! … SLAM! … KRACK! … PUNCH! … POW!

(The SOLDIER straddles TUC and jams the flashlight against TUC's throat.)

BUDDY *(cont'd)*. Terry is down on the ground, almost dead, done for. When … POW!

(The SOLDIER rolls off, bolts and runs.)

BUDDY *(cont'd)*. Terry kicks the Nazi right into next week! *(Stops and checks his watch.)* 10:45 p.m. All quiet! Streets secure! Time to beat it back to bed!

(BUDDY turns and a bright light shines out of the darkness.)

BUDDY *(cont'd)*. Hello? Who's there?

(The light comes closer.)

BUDDY *(cont'd)*. I said, who's there?

(The light comes closer.)

BUDDY *(cont'd)*. Hey, this isn't funny. SPEAK TO ME!

(TUC shines the flashlight onto his own face.)

BUDDY *(cont'd)*. Tuc! You scared the liver out of me!

TUC. Go home!

BUDDY. What happened to your face, Tuc? You got a bloody nose and your eye is all messed up. You been in a fight?

TUC. I said, go home!

BUDDY. Who hit you, Tuc? Was it the prisoner, was it, Tuc?

TUC. NOW!

BUDDY. What did you see, Tuc! Tell me, what did you see?

(BUDDY moves away and lights change.)

TUC. Nothing! No one!
Too dark to see.
A flash of light,
A glance, a glimpse,
I see something that cannot be.

(TUC and VOICE exit.)

SCENE 4

(BUDDY moves downstage into a series of spotlights as four days pass.)

BUDDY. April 6th: Surveillance Report. Tuc got beat up last night. Won't say who did it. Says he fell down. Sounds fishy to me! Old Watch thinks so, too.

April 7th: Sat in the spotter's post for three hours, got splinters in my … self. Saw nothing! Old Watch ate a mouse, whole.

April 8th: Walked around June's house 23 times. Saw footprints, but they were just mine. Thought I heard someone snoring inside, but it was just Old Watch passing gas.

April 9th: Tomorrow I'm going to Dug Hill to check out reports of FOREIGN talk up there. Old Watch going as lookout.

(Lights fade.)

SCENE 5

(Lights up on Dug Hill—morning. NELL sits at the short-wave radio listening and writing information on small cards. BUDDY enters with one end of his rope, that he ties to a nearby tree limb.)

RADIO VOICE *(under the static). Auf acht heute abend werden wir die namen ...*

(BUDDY talks to OLD WATCH who is offstage.)

BUDDY. Now, Old Watch, you gotta stay there and keep quiet. This is surveillance and it's a quiet thing. So, no barking, howling, yipping, growling or farting. Understand?

NELL *(to the radio)*. Come on now … Almost there … Almost … There!

RADIO VOICE *(barely audible through static)*. My name is Robert Spahr, serial number 27681947, arrived in Germany …

NELL *(writes on a small card)*. Robert Spahr …

RADIO VOICE. *Seriennummern und Heimstädte der amerikanischen Soldaten.*

BUDDY. Yikes! There really is someone speaking German.

NELL. Contact information, I need the contact information …

(BUDDY sneaks towards the shack with a notebook. The SOLDIER slips out of the shadows, pulls out a large knife, cuts the rope and exits.)

BUDDY *(copying what he's heard). Oooof accchhhh acchhhhhh ... Amerikanisshhhh ...*

(The radio goes to static again. NELL whacks the side of the radio and the reception is lost completely.)

NELL. BLAST!

(A dog barks furiously.)

BUDDY. Hush! Shhhhh! Old Watch, NO!

(NELL stands up and looks in the direction of BUDDY, who ducks down to avoid being seen. The dog barking triggers the sound of birds screeching.)

NELL *(to the birds)*. Blasted birds! Get out of my garden. Shoo. Shoo!

(NELL steps off the porch and the card she has been writing falls to the ground. NELL exits swiftly into her shack. BUDDY dashes into the clearing, grabs the card and dashes back to where he tied Old Watch.)

BUDDY. Old Watch? Somebody cut this rope!

(NELL comes around the corner of her shack carrying a shotgun. She cocks it and BUDDY whirls around.)

NELL. What are you lookin' at?

BUDDY *(terrified)*. Nothin'

NELL. You call me nothin'?

BUDDY. I'm … I'm … I'm just looking for my dog.

NELL. Your dog?

BUDDY. I uhhhhhh tied him up right over there and now he's gone!

NELL. You see those cow birds down there rampaging around in my garden?

BUDDY. Yes, ma'am.

NELL. What are they doing?

BUDDY. They're hoppin' all over your butter beans and pecking the fool out of your tomatoes.

NELL. Try telling them shoo!

BUDDY. Me?

NELL. Yes, you!

BUDDY *(weakly)*. Shooo, shoo …

NELL. What'd they do?

BUDDY. Nothin'.

NELL. You know what always works for me?

BUDDY. What?

(NELL swings the gun and fires it straight up in the air. BLAM! There is the sound of birds squawking and flying away.)

BUDDY *(cont'd)*. What'd you do that for?

NELL. Just said goodbye to them. Now, young man, goodbye!

(NELL fires in the air again. BLAM! BUDDY turns and races down Dug Hill. Lights change as the sound of the gunshot echoes and reverberates with the sound of machine gunfire.

Lights up on the foxhole. The SOLDIER is pinned down in a firefight. TUC enters carrying a small box of groceries. The SOLDIER continues firing. TUC steps deliberately into the SOLDIER's line of fire. The sound of gunfire stops instantly. TUC puts down the box and backs away slowly. The SOLDIER runs to the box, picks it up and exits. Lights shift.)

SCENE 6

(The store—noon.)

CLOVIS. A loaf of bread, a can of Vienna Sausages, a quart of milk, now don't that beat all!

(MARGARET, a woman in a smart business suit, enters.)

CLOVIS *(cont'd)*. Mornin'

MARGARET. Morning! I just came in on the bus from Jonesboro and I wonder if you could direct me to Abel Crow's garage?

CLOVIS. Yep, one street over on the left!

MARGARET *(starting to exit)*. Thanks!

CLOVIS *(without looking up)*. Except Able's not there.

MARGARET. Do you know where he is?

CLOVIS *(pointing to his map)*. Somewhere in the Philippines.

MARGARET. Actually, I'm looking for someone who works as a mechanic in his shop.

CLOVIS. Tuc?

MARGARET. Yes, Jonas Tucker.

CLOVIS. Most of us are kind of hoping that when Able gets back from overseas, he'll take up another line of work and let Tuc keep doing what he's doin'.

MARGARET. So, he's a good mechanic?

CLOVIS. There's nothing he can't fix. Whether it's a combine or a pocket watch, he's got the gift for anything with gears!

MARGARET. You've known him a long time?

CLOVIS. He started out sweeping floors for me when he was a kid, as more and more people left town for jobs, wars or whatever, Tuc kind of took over whatever needed to be done.

MARGARET. Then I suppose you can vouch for his reliability, trustworthiness and general character?

CLOVIS. What's this all about?

MARGARET. I'm just doing a basic background check, that sort of thing, you know.

CLOVIS. No, I don't know. If you have any more questions, you'll have to ask Mr. Tucker himself. He's out with the mail and should be back directly.

MARGARET. I need to make a telephone call. Do you have a phone I could …

CLOVIS. Out front by the pumps.

(MARGARET exits as BUDDY enters at a run.)

BUDDY. Mr. Eudy. Mr. Eudy …

CLOVIS. Buddy Ricks, I've been looking for you. I called your house and your ma said that you sneaked off at dawn and she was on her way to Jonesboro alone!

BUDDY. Listen! This is important! Acchhhh. Achhhhhh … What does that sound like?

CLOVIS. Sounds like you got phlegm in your throat. Now I've got to have a serious talk with you, young man.

BUDDY. It sounds like GERMAN!

CLOVIS. Buddy …

BUDDY. But that's not all. I went on a reconnaissance mission and I tied up Old Watch and when I turned around, he was gone. The rope was cut … with a KNIFE! Somebody stole my dog. I been lookin' all over town, but he ain't nowhere. Do Germans eat dogs?

CLOVIS. No, 'specially not THAT dog!

BUDDY. But here's the big thing. The really big thing! What does THAT look like to you?

(BUDDY produces the postcard he took.)

CLOVIS. A postcard.

BUDDY. Look at the writing on it!

CLOVIS. It's got a name, and some numbers and, "Arrived in Germany." Buddy, this is very serious!

BUDDY. I know!

CLOVIS. You could get in a lot of trouble!

BUDDY. ME?

CLOVIS. This looks like somebody's mail and tampering with the U.S. mail is a federal offense.

BUDDY. But it says GERMANY! We're at war with Germany!

CLOVIS. I am aware of that, but it's still somebody's mail! Where did you get this?

BUDDY. I found it.

CLOVIS. Where?

BUDDY. Uhhhh, on the ground.

CLOVIS. I suggest that you go back where you found it and see if someone …

BUDDY. But, Mr. Eudy …

CLOVIS. I mean it, Buddy. The mail is serious business.

(BUDDY puts the card in his pocket.)

CLOVIS *(cont'd)*. Now I have something important to talk to you about. I don't mind giving you store credit if you don't have cash money, but I will not tolerate you snitching things.

BUDDY. Snitchin'?

CLOVIS. Someone broke into the store last night and stole some food and a bottle of milk.

BUDDY. It wasn't me!

CLOVIS. Somebody with a key!

BUDDY. BUT …

CLOVIS. They took some milk, a loaf of bread, some wieners …

BUDDY. WIENERS? Mr. Eudy, wieners is German! The POW broke in and stole that stuff.

CLOVIS. No broken windows. No forced entry!

(JUNE enters, upset.)

JUNE. Mr. Eudy, can I use your phone?

CLOVIS. Someone's on it!

JUNE. I've got to call the sheriff. Last night I heard someone outside my window again, and this morning I found these right under the sill.

(JUNE holds cigarette butts and a crumpled package in her hand.)

BUDDY. CIGARETTE BUTTS!

JUNE. I've never seen this brand of cigarettes before. Golli … waaa ssss …

(MARGARET enters.)

MARGARET. Gauloises.

(All turn to stare at her.)

MARGARET *(cont'd)*. I'm sorry, I couldn't help overhearing. The cigarettes are called Gauloises.

BUDDY. That's foreign, ain't it! I bet they're GERMAN.

MARGARET. French.

BUDDY. I told you!

CLOVIS. You said German.

BUDDY. They're still evidence.

MARGARET. Everybody smokes these overseas, mostly soldiers and spies.

JUNE. Spies?

MARGARET. That's what Bogie smoked in *Casablanca.*

BUDDY *(to JUNE)*. First the German breaks into the store and gets himself a little snack. Then he sits down under your window and has himself a smoke. Then he steals my dog! It all makes sense! Don't you see?

CLOVIS. I see someone with an active imagination. June, the phone's free.

(JUNE exits.)

BUDDY. I think it is my duty to warn you, ma'am, that we've got a dangerous prisoner of war escaped around here and it ain't safe for ladies to be traveling alone. Are you lost?

MARGARET. Lost?

BUDDY. Well this town ain't on the way to anywhere else, so if you're here, you gotta be lost!

CLOVIS. She's looking for Tuc.

BUDDY *(astonished)*. TUC? Whatever for?

CLOVIS. Buddy!

BUDDY. I never knew Tuc knew anybody but us!

CLOVIS. You'll have to excuse Buddy, we don't get many strangers around here.

MARGARET. Do you know where he might be?

BUDDY. If he ain't here or at the garage, he might be at the depot, or on his mail route, or pretty much anywhere in town …

MARGARET. Well that certainly narrows it down.

BUDDY. Or he could be up on Dug Hill, he goes there sometimes.

MARGARET. Dug Hill?

BUDDY. You know Dug Hill.

MARGARET. I've … uh heard of it.

BUDDY. There's a graveyard up there with ghosts and spooks. A headless horseman used to ride over the old Jonesboro road, but now it's just a crazy person up there and maybe Nazis. It's just like the Forest of the Ardennes, it could be crawling with Nazis.

MARGARET. How come you know so much about Nazis?

BUDDY. I am a junior lieutenant in the Citizen's Air Corps!

MARGARET. You're adorable!

BUDDY. I am NOT adorable, I'm 11!

(IZZY enters.)

IZZY. Clovis, you'll never guess what I just saw.

CLOVIS. I thought you were off to the war office in Jonesboro this morning?

IZZY. I saw something that made me turn right around and hightail it back here. I was driving right behind the Jonesboro bus and you know how it always slows down when it passes the POW camp in Pomona? Well this time it stops, and you will never guess who gets off and goes right into that camp. They let her right through the barbed wire and everything …

CLOVIS. Who?

IZZY. Nell Hicks!

(MARGARET looks up.)

BUDDY. GAW! That's where I heard German early this morning, up there on Witch Mountain!

IZZY. Buddy, I told you NEVER to go up there.

BUDDY. She shot off a gun and I got out of there quick.

IZZY. She shot at you?

BUDDY. Not AT me, just in the air.

IZZY. What cause does Nell Hicks have to be visiting a German POW camp and shooting guns at children?

BUDDY. I was kind of trespassing.

MARGARET. Did you say Nell Hicks?

IZZY. I did.

MARGARET. Does she still live around here?

IZZY. She does.

BUDDY. She lives up on Witch Mountain.

IZZY. I'm Izzy Sue, and you are?

MARGARET. Margaret, Margaret Briley.

IZZY. Might I ask how you know Nell Hicks?

(Sound of an airplane buzzing the store. JUNE enters at a run.)

JUNE. Mr. Eudy, there's an airplane heading right for …

IZZY. Lands, Lord Almighty!

CLOVIS. An airplane?

(BUDDY races up to the spotter's post.)

BUDDY. I'm on it, Mr. Eudy!

JUNE. I thought it was going to crash right into us and then it pulled up again!

(The plane buzzes again.)

CLOVIS. Buddy, do you have a positive ID?

BUDDY. Inverted gull wing position, single engine, double cockpit and a GREAT BIG SWASTIKA ON THE TAIL. It's a STUKA DIVE BOMBER!

IZZY. OH, MY LORD!

CLOVIS. Buddy, hit the siren!

(The siren wails. The plane buzzes again. ALMA enters at a run.)

ALMA. Clovis, what in the world is going on?

CLOVIS. Take cover, Alma, we're under attack!

ALMA. Attack?

CLOVIS.That plane is a Stuka dive bomber, one of the deadliest fighters in the war!

ALMA. What is it doing in Illinois?

CLOVIS. Civil Air procedure says for you to take cover immediately!

BUDDY. It's climbing, Mr. Eudy.

(Everyone but ALMA dives for cover.)

ALMA. This is Illinois, how could it possibly …

CLOVIS. I am the air raid warden of this town and if I tell you to take cover …

BUDDY. Climbing …

ALMA. A German plane in the middle of the U.S., in the middle of Illinois?

CLOVIS. I do not need a geography lesson, but I do need everyone to take cover, immediately!

BUDDY. PARACHUTE! Mr. Eudy, someone just jumped out of that plane and the plane is flying away.

CLOVIS. What?

IZZY. Buddy, you come down from there!

(Everyone races out into the street and looks up.)

MARGARET. There it is!

BUDDY. I've never seen a real live parachute before. WOW! OH WOW!

CLOVIS. This is NOT a joking matter! That man could have a weapon!

IZZY. Oh, my Lord! Oh, my Lord!

CLOVIS. Everyone, get down!

(A figure enters dragging the strings of a huge parachute. CLOVIS shoulders his rifle.)

CLOVIS *(cont'd)*. On behalf of the United States government and according to the terms of the Geneva Convention, I hereby inform you that you are under arrest and that you are now a prisoner of war.

(The figure stands up.)

CLOVIS *(cont'd)*. Do not attempt to escape!

(The figure whips off the helmet and goggles. Her long hair reveals her identity as GIRL.)

GIRL. Well, in that case, Mr. Eudy, I guess I'll just have to surrender!

CLOVIS, ALMA & IZZY. IT'S GIRL!

(BUDDY runs and leaps into her arms. She spins him around.)

END OF ACT I

ACT II

SCENE 1

(Split stage. On one side is ALMA's porch, where BUDDY sits with GIRL. On the other, the foxhole, where the SOLDIER crouches. Sounds of gunfire.)

SOLDIER. RUN!

(Explosion.)

SOLDIER *(cont'd)*. I can't see you! I can't hear you! I CAN'T HEAR ANYTHING!

GIRL *(simultaneous with SOLDIER)*. I can't hear anything …

(Lights down on the foxhole.)

… because the cockpit is open and the wind is whipping, and the sound of the anti-aircraft shells are so loud. POW … BLAM … BOOM … they make my teeth rattle. They're so close I can smell the creosote and gunpowder!

BUDDY *(spellbound)*. They're shooting at you?

GIRL. That's the whole point.

BUDDY. Trying to hit you?

GIRL. Trying to hit the target sock I'm dragging about 20 feet behind the plane. So, I yank the joystick and pull my P-52 in a steep bank … YEOOOOOWWWWWW … BOOM, another shell, right off my left wing.

BUDDY. What if they hit you?

GIRL. They win. I lose!

(ALMA enters with lemonade and cookies.)

ALMA. Are you filling that boy's head with wild tales?

GIRL. Tryin' to!

ALMA. What were you doing flying in a German dive bomber?

GIRL. Friend of mine was flying it to Chicago to put in some museum, so I asked if I could tag along.

BUDDY. Did you ever shoot anyone down?

GIRL. We didn't even have ammo! They just used us for target practice and dogfights. Man, that's what I wanted to do. Just once to put a P-47 into a death spiral just to see what it felt like!

BUDDY. You know, we got some excitement of our own going on here. We got ourselves a genuine German on the loose, a dangerous escaped prisoner of war!

GIRL. So I hear.

BUDDY. He's probably holed up in the woods somewhere biting the heads off squirrels and eating them raw.

ALMA. Buddy!

BUDDY. He stole my dog. He stole Old Watch!

GIRL. That's Ricky's dog. He was always running off, every chance he'd get.

BUDDY. This time's different. I tied him up with a rope and it got cut with a knife.

GIRL. Ricky always said, just leave him alone and he'll come home.

BUDDY. If I had your plane, I could find that German! *(Starts zooming around like a plane.)* First, I'd nail him with my Browning 75 millimeter nose turret machine gun. *(Fires an imaginary machine gun.)* Then I'd bomb him from a B-24 Liberator … *(Makes the sounds of bombs dropping and exploding.)*

ALMA. Buddy, could you drop your bombs … over there?

(BUDDY moves a bit away.)

GIRL. So, Alma, how's the mortuary business?

ALMA *(deadpan)*. Dead.

GIRL. Alma!

ALMA *(bursts out laughing)*. Oh, Lord, Girl, you have no idea how long I've been waiting to say that.

(GIRL bursts out laughing, too.)

ALMA *(cont'd)*. I've just been hoping somebody would ask me.

(They share a ridiculous moment.)

GIRL. I was sorry to hear about your job at the plant. June told me they've been laying off people left and right.

ALMA. Just the women.

GIRL. That's not fair.

ALMA. Two shifts! I was pulling two shifts, back to back, popping rivets into airplane wings, BAM, BAM, BAM. Lord, I loved that rivet gun!

GIRL. Alma, I do believe wartime has made you spunky!

ALMA. God only knows how long Hosiah will be gone, and business is so slow around here we haven't had a funeral in a dog's age. There's nobody left in this town, even to die!

GIRL. What will you do?

ALMA. Make do. That's what we all do around here, we just keep making do until we don't. Girl, after the war, you could always come back here. Your old room is always ready for you.

GIRL. Alma, I left this town long before I was gone.

(BUDDY zooms back.)

BUDDY. You could come back! I could go with you when you fly, just like when you used to take me dust cropping!

GIRL. Crop dusting! I don't think so, Buddy!

(TUC enters on his bike and ringing his bell. TUC gets off his bike and rolls it to VOICE, who enters and catches it. GIRL leaps up to hug TUC.)

GIRL *(cont'd)*. TUC! Did you see me? Buzzing and buzzing and buzzing the town?

(Together they dive bomb in sign language. TUC makes an elaborate display out of her parachute drop. GIRL signs and speaks.)

GIRL *(cont'd)*. Who else would come dropping down out of the sky?

TUC. It's good to see you, Girl!

GIRL. I got your message and I come as quick as I could!

(CLOVIS enters holding a small box. He crosses to TUC.)

CLOVIS. There you are, Tuc! I been looking all over tarnation for you. Telegram came in over to the depot and they sent it right over to me. I didn't think it could wait for you to get back.

BUDDY. Who's it for?

CLOVIS. Buddy, is your momma home?

BUDDY. Give it to me. I can take it to her.

CLOVIS. Please go get your mother.

BUDDY *(shouting)*. MA! MA! Mail's here!

(IZZY enters from her porch.)

IZZY. I'm coming, son!

BUDDY *(shouting)*. HURRY UP, MA, it's a …

IZZY. I can hear you, Buddy … I'm not de … *(Notices TUC and stops.)* I expect you have something for me, Tuc.

CLOVIS. Actually, Izzy, I do.

IZZY. Clovis! What are you …

CLOVIS. This just came in over the wire at the depot. I couldn't find Tuc, so I brought it myself. It's from the war department.

BUDDY *(shouting)*. June! June! We finally got a telegram! We finally heard something from …

ALMA *(wary)*. Buddy …

(JUNE enters from her porch.)

JUNE. What is it, Buddy?

BUDDY. Maybe they found Ricky, maybe he's coming home, maybe it's good news. Maybe it's …

(IZZY rips it open. She reads in silence.)

IZZY. No, Buddy, it's not.

(She holds the telegram out to ALMA, who takes it gently.)

ALMA. They've changed Ricky's status from missing to …

BUDDY. What?

(ALMA turns away and TUC can't see her lips.)

ALMA. Killed. Killed in action.

BUDDY. Momma?

IZZY *(words fail her)*. Buddy … I … I …

(GIRL turns to JUNE, ALMA to IZZY, everyone starts talking at once. TUC tries to get someone's attention to no avail.)

GIRL. Oh, June, I'm sorry … I'm so, so …

ALMA. Izzy, oh, Izzy.

IZZY. Oh, sweet Lord!

CLOVIS. My sincerest …

BUDDY. I don't believe it! I still don't …

TUC. What does it say?

JUNE. I was so afraid …

TUC *(trying to get her attention)*. Girl! Girl! What does it say?

JUNE. After all this time, all this waiting …

IZZY. Oh, June …

TUC *(stamps on the ground)*. TELL ME!

GIRL *(speaks and signs)*. Ricky's dead.

(ALMA shows him the telegram.)

TUC. It's not right.

GIRL. Of course it's not right.

ALMA. Boys dying in action is never right.

BUDDY. So, where's his body?

GIRL. Buddy, they may never …

BUDDY. I won't believe it until I see his body.

ALMA. It was winter …

BUDDY. In a coffin!

GIRL. Buddy …

BUDDY. Covered with a flag!

(BUDDY runs off. TUC starts after him.)

CLOVIS. The Army sent back Ricky's duffle and this box.

GIRL. You take the box. I'll get the duffle.

(TUC exits with the box.)

IZZY. What are we going to do, June?

JUNE. Come into my house. I'll make us some tea.

(JUNE and IZZY exit.)

GIRL. Where's the duffle, Mr. Eudy?

CLOVIS. Over to the depot. I'll go with you.

ALMA. I expect they'll be wanting a service. I'd best be ready.

(GIRL, ALMA and CLOVIS exit. Lights up on TUC and VOICE.)

TUC. A soldier leaves.
A box comes home.
It isn't fair. It isn't right.
But I have sworn
And I keep my promises without fail.
I bring the mail.

SCENE 2

(A quiet place. Lights up on BUDDY. TUC enters. VOICE stands a short distance away in shadow and voices for TUC.)

TUC.You OK?

(BUDDY turns away. TUC puts the box in front of him.)

BUDDY. That's Ricky's stuff, isn't it? The Army sent it back?

TUC. Do you want to open it?

BUDDY. No!

TUC. OK.

BUDDY. It doesn't prove anything.

TUC. OK.

BUDDY. You open it.

TUC. OK.

(TUC opens the box. BUDDY peeks in.)

TUC *(cont'd)*. Here's a bunch of letters.

BUDDY. I bet some of them are from me, but I'll bet most are from June, she wrote him everyday, even after …

TUC. And a wallet.

BUDDY. He got that from Mama for Christmas last year.

TUC. It's full of pictures.

BUDDY. Any of me?

(TUC shows him one.)

BUDDY *(cont'd)*. That's me with watermelon seeds for teeth! I stuck them on with … never mind. It was kind of disgusting. *(Finds several medals.)* Hey look, there's medals in here. *(Pulls them out.)* Here's his Good Conduct Medal. He showed me that one when he was home on leave before he shipped out. That's a Combat Rifleman Badge and a Bronze Star … Look at this one …

(TUC draws a heart on BUDDY's chest.)

BUDDY *(cont'd)*. Purple Heart.

TUC. Ricky is a … *(Finger spells.)* H. E. R. O. Hero.

BUDDY. I know. But I'd rather he was … *(Finger spells.)* H. E. R. E. Here. *(Beat.)* It's so strange, everything here is just like always and we get this telegram and the whole world is different …

TUC. Ricky isn't gone!

BUDDY. That's what I don't understand. How can someone be here one minute, and then all of a sudden, they're just … gone.

TUC. He is here … *(Pointing to BUDDY's head.)* He is here … *(Pointing to BUDDY's heart.)* Ricky is HERE!

BUDDY. I don't understand.

(Lights change. VOICE and TUC are in a spotlight.)

TUC. So much to say.
But cannot speak.
I have promises to keep
And secrets buried deep.

SCENE 3

(Interlude.

A moment of pause and heartbreaking simplicity.

Perhaps there is a drum, perhaps not.

Lights come up on the windows of JUNE's and IZZY's houses.

JUNE and IZZY change the blue stars in their windows to gold.

That's all.)

SCENE 4

(Lights up on the store. BUDDY is filling a bag with provisions. CLOVIS enters.)

BUDDY. Chocolate bars, graham crackers, peanut butter, flashlight, batteries.

CLOVIS. Mind telling me what you're doing?

BUDDY. Getting provisions. Two bottles of Yoo-hoo and one pickled egg. There! I figure that will be about $1.93 and two ration stamps.

(BUDDY pays CLOVIS.)

CLOVIS. What's this about?

BUDDY. When Ricky left he told me I was in charge of keeping things safe here at home. He said I was the man in the house and Mama and June were my responsibility; so, I'm going after the German!

CLOVIS. The German?

BUDDY. It ain't safe here as long as he is on the loose!

CLOVIS. You leave this to the adults.

BUDDY. Mr. Eudy, it's been almost a week and the adults haven't done NOTHIN'!

CLOVIS. Go home. Your mother needs you at home.

BUDDY. Momma and June just sit on the sofa and as soon as one of them stops crying, the other one starts. People keep coming by with casseroles. I gotta get out of the house. They already took down our blue star and put up a gold one.

CLOVIS. I'm sorry about Ricky, Buddy. I truly am.

BUDDY. I just don't believe it, Mr. Eudy. I don't think I ever will.

CLOVIS. You know, after I lost my Virgie Jewel, I set a place for her at dinner every night for almost a year.

BUDDY. Really?

CLOVIS. And sometimes, I'd even talk to her.

BUDDY. Did she ever answer you back?

CLOVIS. First time in all our married life, she didn't. Now come on, Buddy, why don't you help me … count peanuts.

(GIRL enters.)

GIRL. Hey, Mr. Eudy!

CLOVIS. Hey, Girl!

GIRL. Hey, Buddy!

BUDDY. Hey.

CLOVIS. Buddy and I are counting peanuts.

(CLOVIS and BUDDY each have a pile of peanuts in their laps. As BUDDY counts, he tosses the peanuts into a smaller bowl on the counter.)

GIRL. I just dropped the duffle off on your front porch, Buddy.

BUDDY. 1, 2, 3, 4 …

GIRL. I'd have taken it inside, but the door was locked.

BUDDY. Ma's over at the … she's talking to Mz. Ward about the … You know.

GIRL. Buddy, if you want to talk or …

BUDDY. 12, 13 …

(CLOVIS and GIRL exchange looks.)

GIRL. I gotta get some things to take up to Dug Hill.

CLOVIS. Help yourself. Leave the money in the till.

BUDDY. I'd be careful if I was you, there's some pretty strange stuff happening up on Witch Mountain.

GIRL. It's Dug Hill, Buddy! Don't you ever call it that … not to me.

BUDDY. Dang it, Girl! You made me lose count. Now I gotta start all over again! 1, 2, 3, 4, 5 …

(MARGARET enters.)

MARGARET. There are only three streets in this town and I have been up and down every one of them four times and I still haven't found him.

CLOVIS. You still looking for Tuc?

BUDDY. 14, 15, 16 …

GIRL *(to CLOVIS)*. Clovis, is this the lady you were telling me about?

(CLOVIS nods.)

GIRL *(cont'd, a little too loud, deliberately)*. The one who's been snooping about …

MARGARET. I beg your pardon?

BUDDY. 18, 19, 20, 21 …

GIRL. Asking all sorts of questions about Tuc?

CLOVIS. I just said she was looking …

GIRL. Asking if he's a good mechanic and if he's honest and trustworthy and reliable …

BUDDY. 31, 36, 44 …

CLOVIS. Looking, not snooping …

MARGARET. Yes, Jonas Tucker, I've been trying to …

GIRL *(whirls to face her)*. Well, let me tell you, not only is he a good mechanic, a GREAT mechanic, he is the most honest, reliable, trustworthy person on the planet …

BUDDY. 77, 89, 136 …

GIRL. And just because he's deaf, doesn't mean that he is any less …

MARGARET.Whoa … whoa …

GIRL. Capable or smart or …

MARGARET. I was just …

GIRL. And you'll have to answer to me if you want to give him ANY trouble!

MARGARET. I don't want to give him any trouble. I want to give him a job!

(BUDDY stops counting.)

GIRL. A job?

CLOVIS. A job?

MARGARET. A job! My name is Magaret Briley. I work for the Goodyear Company as a personnel officer in charge of Deaf recruitment. I go all over this part of the country trying to find skilled Deaf workers for Goodyear. With so many servicemen gone, there are jobs, good jobs, high pay, benefits, everything!

BUDDY. Tuc's got a job.

GIRL. How did you hear about Tuc?

BUDDY. He's got about two or three jobs!

MARGARET. He applied for a position as a mechanic.

GIRL. He did?

BUDDY. HE DID?

MARGARET. We got his application in Jonesboro, but the opening's in our Akron plant.

BUDDY. Where's Akron? *(Begins dropping the peanuts out of his lap.)*

MARGARET. It's a great Deaf community.

CLOVIS. Buddy, you're dropping the peanuts …

BUDDY. Where's Akron?

CLOVIS. They're spilling all over the place.

MARGARET. Look, this is a once in a lifetime opportunity, once in a lifetime, and it's going to go to somebody else if I don't find him before I catch the last bus back to Jonesboro tonight!

BUDDY. WHERE'S AKRON????

GIRL. It's in Ohio.

CLOVIS. About 500 miles away!

GIRL. He'd have to leave here.

BUDDY. Tuc's leaving? *(Jumps up, scattering the peanuts.)*

CLOVIS. Mind the peanuts …

BUDDY. Everything in my whole life disappears and you think I care about a bunch of stupid peanuts?

(BUDDY throws down the peanut bowl and storms out.)

CLOVIS. I better get the broom.

(CLOVIS exits.)

MARGARET. I'm sorry if I …

GIRL. It's not your fault. Buddy's brother's been MIA overseas. We just found out that he's not coming back.

MARGARET. I'm so sorry.

(CLOVIS enters, hands GIRL a broom and dustpan, and exits.)

GIRL. First gold star in Ware! I thought we might get through the whole war without one. Sorry if I jumped down your throat, but Tuc's like my big brother, always lookin' out for me. When I was growing up, some people, even some people here, weren't always very nice to him.

(MARGARET and GIRL clean up the mess together.)

MARGARET. So, have you known Tuc a long time?

GIRL. All my life. *(Signing.)* Taught me to sign and everything.

MARGARET *(signing)*. You know sign language?

GIRL *(signing)*. Yeah, I used to call them air pictures!

MARGARET. What's your name?

GIRL. Don't have one.

MARGARET. Everybody has a name.

GIRL. Well actually, I've had a bunch of names, but none of them seem to stick. So they just call me Girl. Names slide right off me like rain off a roof.

MARGARET. That's terrible.

GIRL. No, it's great. I get to make myself up all over again every time I fly off to another place.

MARGARET. What about your family?

GIRL. I was raised by every woman in this town and every one of them gave me something different, but none of them could ever give me a name that stuck.

MARGARET. You're an orphan?

GIRL. Orphan child of an orphan child, or so the story goes, dropped off on a doorstop like so much laundry!

(GIRL exits to empty the dustpan.)

MARGARET *(cont'd.)* How old are you?

GIRL *(offstage)*. Twenty-three.

MARGARET *(reels a bit)*. Twenty-three? Are you sure?

GIRL *(offstage)*. I may not know my own name, but I am pretty sure I know how old I am.

(GIRL enters. MARGARET is flustered.)

MARGARET. Oh my … Ohhhh, my, my, my, my, my …

GIRL. Are you OK?

MARGARET. No! Yes! I mean … I'm fine.

GIRL. If I see Tuc, I'll tell him you're looking for him.

MARGARET *(impulsively pulls out a business card)*. This is my card … here, take two, keep one for yourself and, uh, if you ever get to Akron, look me up. I'm always looking for someone … who can sign.

(MARGARET exits in a hurry. Lights change.)

SCENE 5

(The road. TUC enters with VOICE. BUDDY enters and runs smack into TUC.)

BUDDY. So, when were you going to tell me?

TUC. Tell you what?

BUDDY. You know, you know perfectly well!

TUC. Slow down.

BUDDY. Or maybe you weren't! Maybe you were just going to up and leave. I'd wake up one morning and you'd be gone …

TUC. I can't read your lips if you …

BUDDY. I thought you were different! I thought we were friends … You were going to leave here and not even tell me! *(Deliberately turns away.)*

TUC. Don't turn away from me!

(TUC takes BUDDY by the shoulders and turns him to face him. BUDDY puts his hands in front of his mouth so TUC can't read his lips.)

BUDDY. BLAH, BLAH, BLAH, BLAH, BLAH!

TUC *(pulling BUDDY's hands away firmly)*. Tell me what is wrong!

BUDDY. First Ricky, then Old Watch, now YOU! Go ahead and GO!

(BUDDY exits.)

TUC. Stop! Wait! Buddy!

VOICE *(signs and speaks directly to TUC)*. It's no use. He won't listen.

(Lights change.)

SCENE 6

(Lights up on Dug Hill. NELL is lying face down on the ground. GIRL approaches carrying groceries. GIRL drops the groceries and runs to her.)

GIRL. Nell! Nell!

NELL. Hesh a minute!

GIRL. Are you all right?

NELL. I said, hesh! I'm listening!

GIRL. To what?

NELL. The ground!

GIRL. You're listening to the ground?

NELL. Well, I can't hear a thing with you jaw-jacking.

GIRL. Why on earth are you listening to the ground?

NELL. When Tuc was just a kid, we planted this garden together; he made me listen to the ground to see if it wanted to be plowed. Now I'm listening to see if it wants to go fallow.

GIRL. What are you listening for?

NELL. A sound like the soil is tired and wants to rest, a sound like the roots are letting go, a sound maybe like a sigh.

GIRL. Well, what does it say?

NELL. I don't know. The turnips aren't talking.

(NELL uses her walking stick to stand. GIRL notices.)

GIRL. I brought you some groceries.

NELL. Don't need any groceries.

GIRL. Just some eggs, milk and a little coffee.

NELL. Don't need any coffee.

GIRL. But you love coffee.

NELL. I already said goodbye to it.

(GIRL exits into the house with groceries.)

GIRL. How are you, Nell?

NELL *(sharply)*. Fine. And if I say I'm fine, I'm fine!

(GIRL re-enters and sits on the edge of the porch. Something under the porch nips her on the back of her heel.)

GIRL. OWWWW! Nell, I think something bit me.

NELL. Where?

GIRL. Under the porch! Something under your porch nipped me on the heel.

NELL *(slams her stick down on the porch)*. Damn it, Delano. You be respectful of my company.

GIRL. Delano?

NELL *(shouting under the porch)*. That is the last straw! Don't you hiss at me, or growl, or make those nasty little clicking noises!

GIRL. Delano?

NELL. Tuc brought him in from the highway after he got hit by a car. I healed him up all right, but now he thinks he owns the place! *(Shouting under the porch.)* Delano, you know my rules, once you're healed you got to go!

GIRL. How long has Delano …

NELL. Two years! I can't get rid of him!

GIRL. What, may I ask, IS Delano?

NELL. Opossum.

GIRL. A possum?

NELL. Opossum. He's mighty particular about the O. Tuc named him Delano after the president. Tuc thinks he favors him around the eyes.

GIRL. Can I see him? *(Peeking under the porch.)* Peuw! Nell. He's stiff as a board and smells terrible. That thing's dead.

NELL. Opossums are mighty crafty that way. They roll over, stiffen up and turn their eyeballs backside out whenever danger's near. They even stink like somethin' foul. When it passes, they pop up good as new.

GIRL *(stands and looks around)*. This place looks just like it did when I stayed with you! You still got your garden. And the house and the yard and all the cages for your critters. You still got my shortwave radio right here on the porch where I left it. I swear time flies forward everyplace on this planet, but right here it stands stock still.

NELL. I got all the pictures of your airplanes you sent me tacked up on my wall.

GIRL. Oh, Nell, I wish I could take you flying with me. Up there in the sky, it's like your whole self comes together. I was born on the wind and I've spent my whole life trying to get back up in the air.

NELL. Why are you here?

GIRL. Actually, Nell, I don't know. Tuc sent me a message telling me to …

NELL. I told him to leave well enough alone and he promised me he would! The winter was hard, that's all. The river flooded out the farmland at The Bottoms' and a lot of trees came down.

GIRL. For pity's sake, Nell, when are you going to move to town?

NELL. Never.

(TUC enters on his bike, his basket is filled with groceries. VOICE enters.)

NELL *(cont'd)*. Tuc, you gotta do something about Delano! He bit Girl.

GIRL. Just a nip!

(GIRL signs as she speaks. NELL uses home sign when she speaks to TUC.)

NELL. He's got to go, Tuc. I mean it. He can't be dependent on me, on us, not after all this time, not now! You gotta take him this afternoon.

TUC. I brought you some groceries.

NELL. You two keep this up and I'm going to have to move out of my house to make room for the dry goods.

TUC. You need to eat!

NELL. I eat!

TUC. I need to borrow some things.

NELL. What kind of things?

TUC. I need blankets, socks and something for a dog bite!

NELL. You got bit by a dog?

TUC. Not me. Someone else. I wouldn't ask if it wasn't important! I need them right away, please!

NELL. I gotta get them from the house.

(NELL exits into the house.)

TUC. Girl, we've got to talk fast. There are things going on here you need to know about.

GIRL. I know about the job, Tuc.

TUC. The job?

GIRL. The one in Akron.

TUC. How do you know about that?

GIRL. That lady, Margaret, she told me all about it. You got it, Tuc! You got the job.

TUC *(disbelief)*. I got the job?

GIRL. But you've got to go right to town, right now.

TUC *(it sinks in)*. I got the job!

GIRL. She's been looking for you all day!

TUC *(excited)*. I got the job!

NELL *(pokes her head out the door)*. Do you need one blanket or two?

TUC. Two.

NELL. Next time I come out here, I want to see that opossum out from under my porch.

(NELL tosses out two small blankets and goes back in the house.)

TUC. There's something else! I need to talk to you about something important.

GIRL. You gotta go now, Tuc. That woman is leaving on the Jonesboro bus tonight and you gotta tell her something, even if it's "no."

TUC. There is something I have to do first!

GIRL. I'll take Delano. I'll take him into the woods and let him go. Don't let this slip away by doing NOTHING!

TUC. I have to take these blankets and …

GIRL. I'll take them for you. Who are they for?

TUC. I can't tell you!

GIRL. Why not?

TUC. I promised!

GIRL. Give me those blankets and get your backside down that hill.

TUC. Leave them on the stump at the campsite in the woods on the west slope of Dug Hill. Just leave them there, walk away and be careful.

(NELL enters.)

NELL. Girl, how long are you staying?

GIRL. I don't know … a day or so.

NELL. Well you better stay down in town, 'cause I just gave away your blanket!

GIRL *(to TUC)*. GO!

(TUC crosses to VOICE as lights change.)

TUC. What to do? I don't know.

(TUC turns to VOICE as if for an answer.)

VOICE *(signs and speaks directly to TUC)*. I don't know!

(Lights change.)

SCENE 7

(The road—late afternoon. TUC rides his bike. MARGARET enters, stands in the middle of the road and waves her arms. TUC screeches to a stop. VOICE enters. MARGARET signs in ASL and speaks. TUC signs. VOICE speaks.)

MARGARET. I guess the only way to find you is to stand in the middle of the road until you run me down!

TUC. Do I know you?

MARGARET. I certainly know you, Tuc.

TUC. You know my name sign! How do you know my name sign?

MARGARET. Jonas Tucker Jr. In town they call you Tuc.

TUC. Who are you?

(MARGARET hands TUC her card.)

MARGARET *(finger spelling her name and giving her name sign for "Margaret")*. Margaret. Name sign … Margaret. Personnel officer in charge of Deaf recruiting for the Goodyear Company.

TUC. I can't take the job.

MARGARET. Wait, at least let me tell you …

TUC. Thank you for coming all this way, but …

MARGARET. At the Goodyear plant in Akron, we have more than 7,000 Deaf workers.

TUC. Seven thousand?

MARGARET. That's more people than are in this whole town and ALL of them are Deaf. We've got Deaf churches, Deaf social clubs, even Deaf Bingo. There is a boarding house that has nothing but Deaf families.

TUC. A whole house?

MARGARET. We even have a Deaf football team, the Goodyear Silents! Everyone in our community is just like you. Everyone signs!

TUC. I teach people here some signs! I read their lips!

MARGARET. How much of what they say do you understand?

TUC. Some, a little, enough!

MARGARET. How much of what you say do they understand?

TUC. Some, a little …

MARGARET. Can you share with them what you see, what you think, what you feel?

TUC. This is my home.

MARGARET. Deaf is your world! *(Beat.)* Why did you apply for this job?

TUC. Sometimes I am lonely.

MARGARET. Sometimes we're all lonely, but when you are lonely all the time, it just seems … normal. When was the last time you even saw another Deaf person?.

(TUC looks at VOICE and signs to him.)

TUC. When I was a boy, I made up a friend who lived in my mirror. I could sign to him and he could sign back to me …

(VOICE joins him in signing.)

TUC *(cont'd)*. And he always understood me, perfectly.

(VOICE steps into shadow but continues to voice for TUC.)

MARGARET. So, you haven't even seen another Deaf person since you left the Deaf school?

TUC. How did you know I went to the Deaf school?

MARGARET. It was in your application.

TUC. No, it wasn't.

MARGARET. I just assumed …

TUC. Why did you come all this way?

MARGARET. I told you, I …

TUC. You couldn't find a Deaf mechanic in Akron?

MARGARET. It's a once in a lifetime opportunity.

TUC. Why me? Why me!

MARGARET. To give you something you never had. To pay you back. To say thank you the only way I know how. You don't recognize me, do you, Tuc? You were just a little boy when I left and I was just a teenager. That was 23 years ago.

TUC. Maizie?

MARGARE. Yes.

TUC. Maizie from the Deaf school?

MARGARET. Yes.

TUC. MAIZIE !!!

MARGARET. Yes.

TUC. I thought you'd be in the movies by now.

MARGARET. Me too. But here I am. I came because I wanted to see you again, but you were so angry with me when I left, I wasn't sure that you'd want to see me. I wanted to float down in a bubble like the good witch in *The Wizard of Oz*, grant a wish for you and disappear.

TUC. Come with me to Dug Hill to see your Girl.

MARGARET. No.

TUC. But she's there.

MARGARET. I said, no!

TUC. Don't you want to meet her? At least see her!

MARGARET *(blurts it out)*. I have!

TUC. You have?

MARGARET. I think so. Did she … *(Makes a sign for a parachute.)*

TUC. YES!

MARGARET. YES?

TUC. YES!

MARGARET. Oh, Tuc, she is beautiful and strong and smart and she knows herself, and that is more than I had hoped to hope for.

TUC. Did you tell her who you are?

MARGARET. No. She was mad as a hornet and shouting at me! After 23 years, I couldn't exactly say to her, "Don't yell at me, I'm your mother!"

TUC. Why didn't you tell her?

MARGARET. I was 16 when I left her on that doorstep, and every single day since then, I have played out in my mind what would happen if I ever saw her again; what she'd say, what I'd say. But when she was there, right in front of me, I couldn't say anything. I just blabbered away like an idiot. I gave her my business card!

(TUC pulls out the card GIRL gave him. MARGARET groans.)

TUC. Did you give me this job because of Girl?

MARGARET. I gave you this job because you are a good mechanic! Tonight I have to catch the last bus to Jonesboro and then a train in the morning to Akron.

TUC. Give me one day. I need just one day to decide.

MARGARET. The phone number of my office in Akron is on my card. Have someone call me when you decide.

(MARGARET turns to go.)

TUC *(calls in his own voice)*. Maizie!

MARGARET. Maizie's gone, Tuc. She left a long time ago, but Margaret hopes to see you again … in Akron.

(MARGARET exits. Lights change.)

TUC. Past in one hand.
Future in the other.
I hold them both
And still don't know
which one to choose.

(VOICE signs and speaks to TUC directly.)

VOICE. You know! And you know, you know!

(VOICE exits first. TUC follows.)

SCENE 8

(Twilight. Lights up on the campsite in the woods and the tree stump. GIRL enters with the pile of blankets and a small cage. She puts the blankets on the stump. She moves a distance away. She puts the cage on the ground in the shadows and opens the door.)

GIRL. Go on now, scoot!

(From the other side of the stage, BUDDY enters with his provisions.)

BUDDY *(rehearsing)*. On behalf of the United States government … and the Geneva Conversation … I hereby inform you that you are a prisoner of war.

(Sits on the ground and opens a bottle of Yoo-hoo.)

Surveillance report April 10th, 10:00 p.m.: Old Watch gone! Tuc going, and nobody here is doing ANYTHING to catch a dangerous and most probably German prisoner!

(The SOLDIER enters and crosses to the stump. He looks about, takes the blankets and starts off. GIRL crosses back with the empty cage. She sees the SOLDIER.)

GIRL. Hello?

(The SOLDIER whirls around and grabs his knife.)

GIRL *(cont'd)*. Hey! Take it easy, I'm not going to …

(The SOLDIER flings the blanket at GIRL. She shields herself with the cage. He turns and runs.)

GIRL *(cont'd)*. Stop! Wait! Hold it! I said …

(GIRL drops the cage and takes off after him. BUDDY hears something and whirls around.)

BUDDY. What's that? Hey … Hey …

(The SOLDIER almost runs into BUDDY. BUDDY throws the bottle at the SOLDIER, who ducks under his coat to shield himself.)

SOLDIER. HEY! HEY!

BUDDY *(stammering)*. On behalf, on behalf, on behalf …

(The SOLDIER races off knocking BUDDY to the ground.)

GIRL. BUDDY!

BUDDY. Get him!

GIRL. BUDDY, are you all right?

BUDDY. It's the POW, the prisoner, the GERMAN.

GIRL. Are you hurt?

BUDDY. I'm fine. Did you see him?

GIRL. I saw something, but I'm not sure what.

BUDDY. Let's get him!

GIRL. The only thing we're going to do is to get you to town right now!

BUDDY. Come on!

GIRL. I mean it, Buddy! Right now!

(BUDDY lurches in the direction of the escaping SOLDIER. GIRL yanks him in the opposite direction. They exit. Lights change.)

SCENE 9

(GIRL and BUDDY race to the store.)

GIRL. Mr. Eudy, are you still open?

CLOVIS. I am now!

BUDDY. We saw him! We saw the POW. Call the sheriff. Call the Army! Call somebody. I tried to arrest him, but he knocked me down and run off.

CLOVIS. Are you all right?

BUDDY. I'm fine, but we need to go after him.

CLOVIS. You're not going after anyone! I'm calling the sheriff.

(CLOVIS exits as IZZY enters.)

IZZY. There you are, Buddy!

BUDDY. Momma! I saw the POW!

IZZY. Did you take Ricky's duffle?

BUDDY. Listen to me, Momma! I saw the prisoner.

IZZY. No, you listen to me! Ricky's duffle is gone!

BUDDY. Maybe June's got it.

(JUNE enters.)

JUNE. Got what?

IZZY. Ricky's duffle. Somebody took it. There's nothing on my porch but that blamed dog.

BUDDY. Old Watch?

(ALMA enters.)

ALMA. I found him. I was on my roadkill run and …

BUDDY. OH NO!

ALMA. He's fine! He hopped right in the hearse when I opened the back!

(CLOVIS enters.)

CLOVIS. Sheriff's over in Mound City. Dispatch says they'll send him right over.

BUDDY. Mound City, that's miles away. We gotta do something now!

ALMA. Why?

CLOVIS. Buddy saw the escaped prisoner.

ALMA. Where?

BUDDY. Up on Witch …

GIRL. Buddy!

BUDDY. Dug Hill. That's what I was trying to tell you. That's where I heard the German talk! On Mz. Hicks' radio.

IZZY. You sold her that radio tube, Clovis.

CLOVIS. I did.

BUDDY. That's where I found the postcard, Mr. Eudy, the one that said Germany!

GIRL. Postcard?

BUDDY. She dropped it! I saw her!

IZZY. And I saw her going into that German POW camp with my very own eyes.

GIRL. Nell?

IZZY. Something is going on in this town, and if that woman is doing anything to help escaped German prisoners, we have a right to know!

GIRL. I was just up there. I didn't see …

CLOVIS. Sympathizing with the enemy! That's a federal offense!

IZZY. She's a traitor! That's what she is a …

JUNE *(explodes)*. What is happening to us? Ricky didn't go to war for this! Neighbor against neighbor?

IZZY. June, you of all people should want the truth to come out. Those Germans killed your husband!

JUNE. The war killed my husband!

IZZY. You can all stand around here jaw jacking, but I am going up that mountain and getting Ricky's duffle bag.

ALMA. Now?

GIRL. Tonight?

JUNE. Why?

IZZY. It's all we have left of him, June! It's all we have left!

(Beat.)

CLOVIS. I think we should wait for the sheriff.

BUDDY. That could be hours!

ALMA. Settle down, Buddy. Now, it's been a really hard day and we're all upset.

IZZY. I'm going and I'm going tonight.

GIRL. I'll go with you, but I'd stake my life that there's a logical explanation. *(Exits.)*

ALMA. I'll get the hearse. It's the only thing big enough to hold everyone.

BUDDY. Can I go, too?

ALL. NO!

CLOVIS. It's best you stay here. I'll meet the sheriff down at dispatch and bring him up to Dug Hill.

IZZY. I mean it, son. If you go up that hill, you will be sent to your room for the rest of your life.

(CLOVIS, ALMA, IZZY and JUNE exit. Lights change.)

SCENE 10

(BUDDY is alone in the store. He runs his hand along the counter. He comes to the cash register and rings up a no-sale, causing the drawer to pop open with a cha-king sound. He closes it, opens it, closes it, opens it, closes it, opens it, with a building and wordless fury. He turns to look at CLOVIS' map, and in a single sweep of his hand, tears it down and shreds it to pieces. He buries his head in his hands and sobs.

TUC and VOICE enter. TUC crosses to BUDDY and puts his hand on his shoulder. BUDDY turns and hugs TUC hard. After a beat, he pulls away, still holding the map fragments.)

BUDDY. I was looking for Akron on the map.

TUC. This map is the whole world. It's too big and Akron's too small to be on it … (*Showing BUDDY another map.)* And this map is the U.S. and here is Akron.

BUDDY. Where are we?

TUC *(showing BUDDY another map)*. Now, this map is just Illinois, but we're too small to see. If you follow the river here and find the Jonesboro road here … Where they come together, you see that speck?

BUDDY. Not really.

TUC. That little speck, right there, that's us!

(After a beat.)

BUDDY. You're leaving?

TUC. Maybe.

BUDDY. I don't want you to go. But I see why you'd want to.

TUC. You do?

BUDDY. Who'd want to spend their whole life on a speck too small to see?

(Lights change.)

SCENE 11

(Lights up on Dug Hill. NELL fusses with the radio, there is the sound of static.)

NELL. Blast!

(There is the sound of a car. GIRL enters.)

NELL *(cont'd)*. There you are, Girl. See if you can tune in this radio. President Roosevelt is speaking tonight …

GIRL. Nell, I'm not here alone. Some folks from town want to talk to you.

NELL. Town? I got nothin' to say.

(ALMA, JUNE and IZZY enter.)

JUNE. I am sorry to bother you, Ms. Hicks. May we talk to you for a few minutes?

NELL. Depends on what it's about?

IZZY. We are investigating the POW escape from Pomona!

NELL. What's that got to do with me?

IZZY. Someone said they heard GERMAN being spoken up here on Dug Hill.

NELL. So, have we declared war on a language now?

IZZY. I saw you get off the bus and walk into that German POW camp big as life!

NELL. I expect you did.

IZZY. What cause do you have to go to a POW camp?

NELL. Last I looked, this was still a free country and my business is my business.

IZZY. Not during wartime!

NELL. During ANY TIME ! Years ago you all came rampaging up this hill on some kind of witch hunt. After all these years, I see that nothing has changed at all!

(There is the sound of static from the radio.)

IZZY. And you've got a shortwave radio during wartime!

GIRL. That's my radio. I had it since I was a kid.

RADIO VOICE. *Hier ist Radio Berlin mit dem Programm "Anrufe Nach Hause."*

IZZY. That announcer said BERLIN!

NELL. He did.

IZZY. Transmitting messages on the shortwave radio during wartime is illegal!

NELL. Listening is NOT! Fighting a war over there is bad enough without having to fight one right here at home!

IZZY. Then there's the matter of the duffle. Somebody stole it right off my porch!

NELL. I have no idea what you're talking about!

IZZY. All his things, everything I've got left of him. His clothes. His shaving kit …

JUNE. Gone.

IZZY. Stolen!

ALMA. Izzy, why didn't you just take it inside?

IZZY. I tried to. I tried time after time, and it got heavier and heavier, because I knew if I brought it in the house, I would have to unpack it and I … just … couldn't!

(BUDDY enters with TUC.)

BUDDY. Just a minute, Momma, I got something to say!

IZZY. Buddy! I told you to stay in town.

BUDDY. I can't, Momma. Not till I tell you what I know.

(TUC nods and motions BUDDY forward.)

BUDDY *(cont'd, holding up a postcard)*. Mz. Hicks, when I was up here the other day, I kind of … accidentally on purpose … picked up this postcard you dropped.

NELL. I wondered what happened to that.

BUDDY. I took it!

JUNE. Buddy!

BUDDY. I noticed that the postcard was addressed to a place called Homberg.

IZZY. Homberg is in Germany.

BUDDY. It's also in Illinois. It's in Pope County. Tuc showed me on one of Mr. Eudy's maps. This postcard is addressed to Homberg, Illinois. Tuc told me you send postcards all over the country to names you get over the shortwave radio.

NELL. What if I do? My mail is my private business.

ALMA. Mz. Hicks, are you monitoring the shortwave radio broadcasts? I heard Mrs. Roosevelt talking about this on the radio. All over this country, shortwave operators listen to German propaganda broadcasts and write down the names and serial numbers of Americans captured and held by the Germans.

IZZY. Well, I never …

ALMA. Then they get in touch with families of servicemen, to let them know they're alive. Is that what you were doing?

NELL *(to JUNE)*. I listened for Ricky's name, but I never heard it.

JUNE. I am so sorry we bothered you.

IZZY. I've been half crazy with worry over Ricky.

NELL. I know.

IZZY. I'm sorry. I apologize.

BUDDY. What about me, Mama? Am I confined to barracks?

IZZY. No, son, you did fine. We better get back down to town for supper.

(ALMA, IZZY and BUDDY exit. JUNE lingers a moment.)

JUNE. Thank you. Thank you for listening.

(NELL nods. JUNE exits. Lights change. VOICE enters.)

TUC. Night comes soon and fast.
Empty places at the table
Filled with silences that last.

(VOICE signs and speaks directly to TUC.)

VOICE. The time for secrets is over.
The time for promises is past.

(Lights change.)

SCENE 12

(Dug Hill—later that evening. TUC tends a stew pot on the fire. VOICE stands in shadow watching. NELL adjusts her chair near the radio. GIRL helps her with the chair, laughing.)

GIRL *(laughing)*. The look on her face, the look on Izzy Ricks' face …

NELL. That woman's heart is broken with grief, she does not deserve your laughter.

GIRL. The only thing I don't get is the POW camp. Why were you there?

NELL *(very brusque)*. That's my business.

TUC *(to NELL)*. Tell her. The time for secrets is over.

NELL. You promised!

TUC. I did, but the time for promises is past.

GIRL. Nell?

NELL. At the camp in Pomona, they've got a doctor for the prisoners who were wounded in battle.

GIRL. So, you went to nurse them?

NELL. After the doctor finishes with the prisoners, he sees charity patients: migrant workers, pregnant teenagers and me.

GIRL. You're sick?

NELL. He ran some tests and sent me the results.

GIRL. What did they say?

NELL. Nothin' my body hadn't already told me.

GIRL. You're going to get better, aren't you?

(NELL turns away, leaving the question unanswered.)

GIRL *(cont'd)*. What about a hospital? There's a hospital in Jonesboro.

NELL. Nothin' a hospital can do except annoy me.

GIRL. You should not be up on this mountain.

NELL. This is exactly where I should be. Everyday I've been letting go of things, one at a time. First it was sunrise, so I'd just get up a little later. Then it was coffee, then my garden, and so on and so on. Little by little, I come to know that whatever happens to me, it will be just one more letting go.

GIRL. Tuc, why didn't you tell me about this?

NELL. I made him promise not to. This is exactly what I didn't want. I didn't want you involved in my own little war. My body is having a kind of battle with itself, but I am just at the edge of peace. And I am just waiting for it.

GIRL. I'm going to stay here and help you.

NELL. Don't need any help.

GIRL. But you will.

NELL. Then I'll get some.

GIRL. I am going to ask Alma and June to look in on you.

NELL. If you do, that whole gaggle of geese will be up here clucking.

GIRL. Then I'll stay.

NELL. No. You got flying to do.

GIRL *(vulnerable)*. But I want to …

NELL. What I want is to hold you both inside my mind as you go off to your own lives. Girl, letting go of you is going to be a bit harder than coffee, so we'd best do it quick! *(Turns to TUC and signs as she speaks.)* And letting go of you, Tuc, is impossible, but you got a brand new job in a brand new place.

(TUC is astonished.)

GIRL. How did you know about the job?

NELL. By now you both should know that I know everything. You are taking that job aren't you?

(TUC takes MARGARET's card out of his pocket and hands it to GIRL and signs, "Call her.")

GIRL. You want me to call her?

TUC. Yes.

GIRL. What do you want me to say?

TUC. Tell her yes.

NELL. Good! Now, Tuc, you take Girl to the bus station and see that she gets on the last bus to Jonesboro tonight. Girl, don't forget my radio.

GIRL. I'll tune it in for you.

(GIRL places the radio on the edge of the porch and something catches her eye.)

GIRL *(cont'd)*. Nell, Delano's back.

NELL. Of course. The president's going to speak. Delano always likes to listen to the president.

(GIRL tunes the radio, then turns and hugs NELL a little longer than either of them intends. GIRL exits.)

NELL *(cont'd)*. It's time, Tuc.

(TUC nods. He starts off and then turns back and starts toward her. She looks away and holds up her hand to stop him. They clasp hands briefly and then let go. TUC moves away.

Lights change. TUC and VOICE look at each other. TUC signs, "Finished." VOICE signs, "Finished." Neither sign is voiced. They exit in opposite directions.)

SCENE 13

(Dug Hill—night. Sound of the PRESIDENT'S VOICE on the radio.)

PRESIDENT'S VOICE. "Today we are faced with the pre-eminent fact that if civilization is to survive we must cultivate the science of human relationships."

(Lights up on NELL sitting in her rocking chair, listening to the radio.)

PRESIDENT'S VOICE *(cont'd)*. "We must work together, in the same world, at peace."

(The SOLDIER enters. He drags the duffle behind him.)

NELL. There's stew on the fire. Tuc made it before he left, but I'm not hungry. I've said goodbye to stew.

(The SOLDIER lurches to the firelight and grabs the stew pot in both hands.)

NELL *(cont'd)*. Help yourself.

(The SOLDIER eats ravenously.)

NELL *(cont'd)*. They all think you're dead.

SOLDIER. Maybe I am.

NELL. Maybe you are.

SOLDIER. Did Tuc tell you about me? I made him promise he wouldn't.

NELL. I figured it out for myself. The duffle was the give away. No one in this town would steal a dead boy's duffle bag, Ricky.

RICKY. How do you know who I am?

NELL. I remember when you used to throw rocks at my house. I remember when you looked in my shack and saw all my critters in there peeping at you. You about wet yourself, it spooked you so bad.

RICKY. They used to call you witch.

NELL. They did.

RICKY. They used to say you could make a cow go dry or do a spell to hex someone 50 miles away …

NELL. They did.

RICKY. … or sing to people right before they died.

NELL. I sing all right, but singing never hurts anyone. It just helps them choose whether to stay or go. Do you want me to sing for you, Ricky?

RICKY. Ricky Ricks got killed at the Battle of the Bulge.

(Sounds of battle are heard.)

RICKY *(cont'd)*. When the shell hit, I didn't hear it. That's how you know it's bad. Smoke all around, guys yelling for medics. Gus, right next to me, screaming. Then I see that both his legs are gone. There's another explosion. I wake up in a field hospital. My dog tags are gone. My hands are burned. And I don't know who I am.

NELL. But here you are.

RICKY. They discharged me as Private Ricks from Muncie, Indiana, and sent me back on a cargo plane. When I tell them who I think I am, they tell me Ricky Ricks from Illinois was killed in action. And I think they must be right. Because I know, whoever I am, I'm not the man who left here.

NELL. Your mama, your wife and your brother are about wild with grief.

RICKY. I can't go to them, not yet.

NELL. Why not?

RICKY. I am so scared I'll hurt them. That's why I made Tuc swear not to tell anyone till I'm sure they'll be safe.

NELL. Safe from what?

RICKY. Safe from me. I beat the daylights out of Tuc when he surprised me. He shined a flashlight in my face and all I saw was bombs! I watch my wife through a window and she looks like a stranger. I scared my little brother and my own dog bit me.

NELL. You need help, boy.

RICKY. I can't stop shaking. I can't eat. I can't sleep.

NELL. You need to let it go.

RICKY. That's why I come to you.

NELL. Me?

RICKY. Do you have a spell that will stop it?

NELL. Stop what?

RICKY. The sounds inside my head.

NELL. All I can give you is a hot meal and a place to sleep by the fire.

RICKY. I haven't slept since I left home.

NELL. Then I expect you must be tired.

RICKY. I am. Oh, Lord, I am!

NELL. Then just sit and listen to this radio. Your commander in chief is talking.

RICKY. I can't hear him. I am dead.

NELL. Oh no, you'll heal.

RICKY. How do you know I'll heal?

NELL. Because I'm a witch and I know everything.

(NELL turns up the radio.)

PRESIDENT'S VOICE. "The work, my friends, is peace. More than the end of this war—an end to the beginnings of all wars. Yes, an end forever to this impractical, unrealistic settlement of differences between governments by the mass killing of people."

(RICKY falls asleep. TUC enters holding BUDDY's hand. He motions for BUDDY to go toward NELL.)

BUDDY. Is that the POW?

NELL. Yes. I reckon he's as much a prisoner of war as anyone.

(NELL motions for BUDDY to come closer.)

BUDDY *(gasps)*. Ricky!

NELL. Mind you, don't wake him. He needs his rest. He hasn't slept for years and years and years.

(With an infinite tenderness born of disbelief, BUDDY slowly sits next to his brother and gently touches his shoulder. NELL begins to sing a wordless requiem of loss and hope. RICKY sleeps. NELL sings.)

END OF PLAY

NOTES